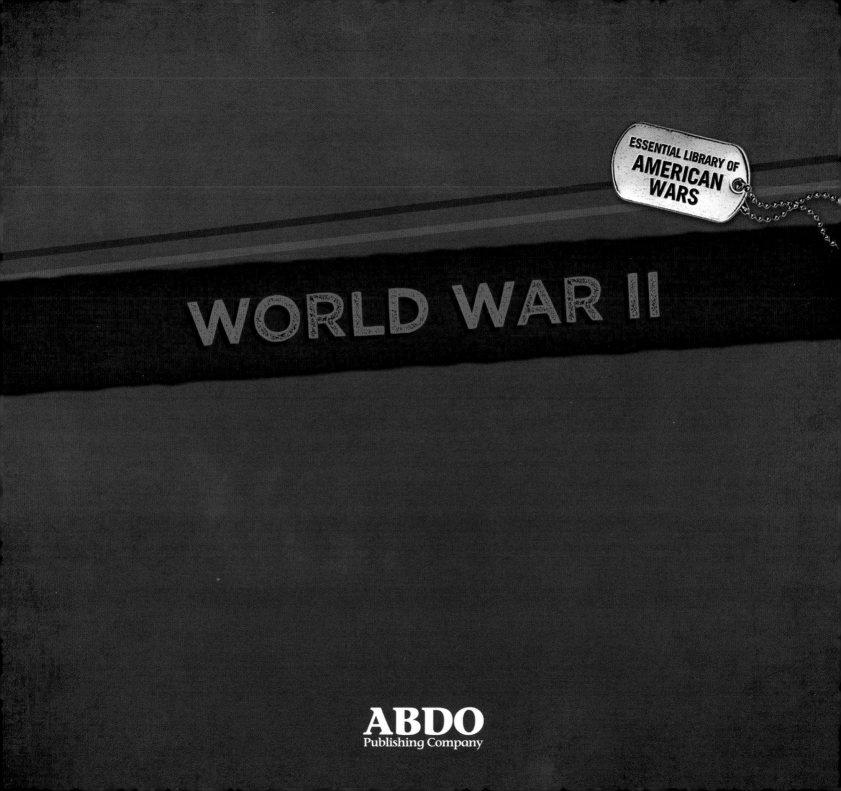

ESSENTIAL LIBRARY OF
AMERICAN
WARS

WORLD WAR II

ABDO
Publishing Company

WORLD WAR II

BY SUSAN E. HAMEN

CONTENT CONSULTANT

G. Kurt Piehler
Institute on World War II and the Human Experience
Florida State University

CREDITS

Published by ABDO Publishing Company, PO Box 398166, Minneapolis, MN 55439. Copyright © 2014 by Abdo Consulting Group, Inc. International copyrights reserved in all countries. No part of this book may be reproduced in any form without written permission from the publisher. The Essential Library™ is a trademark and logo of ABDO Publishing Company.

Printed in the United States of America,
North Mankato, Minnesota
052013
012014

Editor: Arnold Ringstad
Series Designer: Emily Love

Photo Credits

AP Images, cover, 2, 26, 28, 31, 35, 38, 48, 55, 56, 61, 63, 64, 74, 90, 97, 99 (left), 101 (middle left), 101 (bottom left), 101 (middle right), 101 (bottom right); US Navy, 6, 9, 12, 42, 98 (left); National Archives, 14, 73, 79, 98 (right); Getty Images, 18, 32; Bettmann/Corbis/AP Images, 21, 23; Galerie Bilderweit/Getty Images, 45; US Marine Corps/AP Images, 52; Lt. F A Hudson/IWM/Getty Images, 59; Keystone-France/Gamma-Keystone/Getty Images, 67; Library of Congress, 68; United States Coast Guard, 77; Photo12/UIG/Getty Images, 81; Joe Rosenthal/Getty Images, 83; US Air Force/AP Images, 89, 99 (right); Red Line Editorial, 85, 100 (top), 100 (bottom), 101 (top); US Army, 92; Ingram Publishing/Thinkstock, 100

Library of Congress Control Number: 2013932680

Cataloging-in-Publication Data

Hamen, Susan E.
 World War II / Susan E. Hamen.
   p. cm. -- (Essential library of American wars)
Includes bibliographical references and index.
ISBN 978-1-61783-882-8
1. World War, 1939-1945--History--Juvenile literature. 2. World War, 1939-1945--Europe--Juvenile literature. I. Title.
940.53--dc23

2013932680

CONTENTS

DAY OF INFAMY

The morning of December 7, 1941, dawned over the Hawaiian islands. It was a Sunday, a relaxing day for the nearly 60,000 soldiers and sailors stationed at the US military bases at Pearl Harbor on the island of Oahu.[1] Home to the US Pacific Fleet, Pearl Harbor was composed of several different bases. Among them were Hickam Field Army Air Base, Wheeler Field, and the naval base in the middle of Pearl Harbor at Ford Island. All eight battleships regularly stationed at Pearl Harbor were in port that day, moored close together near Ford Island.

A SECRET MISSION

Japan was inching closer to war with the United States. It viewed the US naval fleet at Pearl Harbor as the only power that could stop its domination of East Asia and the Pacific Ocean. As a result of Japan's regional aggression and

Pearl Harbor in the fall of 1941

its alliances with Germany and Italy—two nations at war with the United Kingdom, a US ally—the United States had established embargoes on shipments of oil and other goods to Japan. Now tensions were high between the two countries. Japanese leaders knew furthering their campaigns in East Asia would require taking these supplies by force. At 6:00 a.m. on December 7, 183 fighter planes and bombers began taking off from the flight decks of Japanese aircraft carriers floating approximately 230 miles (370 km) north of Hawaii.[2] Their target: Pearl Harbor.

US radar operators Joseph Lockard and George Elliott were nearing the end of their shift at 6:45 a.m. when they spotted a flicker on their radar screens. It looked as though a few aircraft were coming in from the northeast. They dismissed them as friendly planes. By 7:02, Lockard noticed a blip larger than anything he had seen before. It was now obvious that a mass of aircraft were heading their way. The men called and reported their discovery to the central hub for all the radio stations: "a large number of planes coming in from the north, three degrees east."[3] Lieutenant Kermit Tyler believed the large blip to be B-17s—US bomber aircraft—coming in from the mainland. He assured Lockard, "Well, don't worry about it. It's nothing."[4] There were B-17s coming in from California that morning, but

Crew members on a Japanese aircraft carrier give a send-off
to the pilots departing for Pearl Harbor.

the large radar blip Lockard and Elliot discovered was a group
of Japanese planes.

TORA! TORA! TORA!

As the first wave of Japanese planes neared Oahu, Japanese
commander Mitsuo Fuchida ordered his pilots to prepare for
the attack. He broke radio silence at 7:53 to call out, "Tora! Tora!

SPIES IN HAWAII

The Japanese Navy sent trained spy Lieutenant Takeo Yoshikawa to Hawaii to discover valuable information that would be needed to plan the surprise attack. Under the alias Tadashi Morimura, the 29-year-old spy arrived in Honolulu in March 1941. He rented an apartment overlooking Pearl Harbor and secretly sent information about ship locations and US military schedules back to the Japanese military.

Tora!" meaning, "Tiger! Tiger! Tiger!"[5] The message meant the Japanese airplanes had caught the bases at Pearl Harbor by surprise. Fuchida's pilots broke into separate groups. Each pilot had a specific target. They had memorized the ships' positions as provided by Japanese spies in Hawaii. The three US aircraft carriers in the Pacific Ocean were not in port that day and would be left unscathed. Their absence was among the most fortunate events for the United States in World War II.

The US cruiser *Raleigh* and training ship *Utah* were the first to be torpedoed. The *Raleigh* fired back at the enemy as the *Utah* began to tilt. The battleship *Pennsylvania* was in dry dock for repairs, so the pilot assigned to it decided instead to attack the *Oglala*. The torpedo skimmed under the *Oglala* and smashed into the *Helena*, severely damaging both ships.

CONFUSION

By 8:05, the cruiser *Raleigh* was tipping over from the continued barrage, and two torpedoes hit the battleship *California*. Crew aboard the repair ship *Vestal* fired back. The battleship *Oklahoma* took two torpedoes to its side. Its sleeping sailors scrambled from their bunks as water rushed into the side of the ship. As another torpedo hit, sailors abandoned efforts to return fire in order to evacuate the quickly capsizing vessel. Many sailors were trapped below deck, where water was rushing in as additional torpedoes slammed into the ship's side. The *Oklahoma* rolled over and sank in the shallow waters of the harbor, dooming the sailors trapped within. It had been just eight minutes since the first torpedo hit the *Oklahoma*. With the ship at the bottom of the harbor, 429 of the men who had been stationed onboard were dead.[6]

The battleships *West Virginia* and *Arizona* sustained significant damage from torpedoes and bombs. At 8:08, a Japanese attack bomber dropped an armor-piercing bomb on the *Arizona*, penetrating the deck and igniting hundreds of tons of ammunition and gunpowder. The massive explosion blew the ship up and out of the water, breaking it in two and killing 1,177 men onboard.[7] The dead on the *Arizona* made up approximately half of all US military fatalities on December 7.

The *Oklahoma* slips beneath the waters of Pearl Harbor.

ATTACK ON THE AIRFIELDS

While Japanese bombers attacked US ships in the harbor, another group of Japanese planes headed for the airfields to destroy US planes before they could launch a counterattack. At Hickam Field, enemy bombers hit A-20 attack aircraft along with B-18 and B-17 bombers. The US planes had been packed closely together in order to discourage sabotage, but the arrangement also left them extremely vulnerable to the Japanese bombers. Hundreds of planes were destroyed on the ground. After bombing the airplanes, the Japanese planes fired on the barracks, the mess hall, the movie theater, and the fire station. The unprepared men in these areas fruitlessly tried to fight back, firing pistols at the low-flying planes. A total of 20 men at Kaneohe and 191 men at Hickam were killed.[8] Dozens more died at Wheeler Field.

At 8:40, a second wave of Japanese planes descended upon the burning and sinking ships and scrambling sailors. More bombs were dropped on the ships that were not already completely destroyed. More ships went up in flames and many more lives were lost.

The Japanese planes finally returned to their aircraft carriers at 9:55 a.m. They had succeeded in destroying two battleships and sinking or damaging another 18 US vessels. They also destroyed 169 aircraft and damaged another 159.[9] The United States had endured a devastating loss of 2,403 lives, including 68 civilians. Another 1,178 people were wounded.[10] The Japanese, on the other hand, had lost between 29 and 60 planes and fewer than 100 men.[11]

FIGHTING IN PAJAMAS

Lieutenant Philip Rasmussen was still in his pajamas when Wheeler Field came under attack. Frantically, he and other pilots scrambled to get their P-36 fighters armed, fueled, and in the air. Finally, Rasmussen was airborne. His plane sustained serious damage in the fighting, but he managed to land. When he checked his plane, he found hundreds of holes from Japanese machine gun fire.

AFTERMATH

Although the bombing had ceased, the terror in Pearl Harbor continued after the Japanese planes departed. Sinking ships trapped sailors who struggled to get free. Others found themselves trying to swim to safety in blazing waters. Doctors and nurses rushed to treat hundreds of men who had sustained serious injuries from machine gun fire, shrapnel, and burns. Able-bodied men rushed to create makeshift hospitals out of barracks and schools. Civilians ran to the aid of the military, offering medical attention, carrying water, or donating much-needed blood.

In the sunken *Arizona* and *Utah,* hundreds of sailors waited in pitch-dark compartments, hoping to be cut free and rescued. Most were not. Rescue efforts could not be started until the following day, when a few dozen men were freed from the two ships. Hundreds more died.

The lineup of battleships at Pearl Harbor as photographed from an attacking Japanese aircraft

STORIES FROM THE WAR

Walter Staff, a survivor aboard the *Oklahoma*, remembered the experience of being rescued:

"You lose all track of time. Then we heard some tapping and we figured something was going on. They tapped one-two, one-two. Then we tapped back. . . . We could see a little bit of light. They are cutting away and I am watching the water below us. The water is coming up and they are cutting. I thought the water was going to beat them. . . . Pretty soon they were up above us. . . . The door flops open and there's your rescue party."[12]

AT WAR

The United States was horrified when reports of the attack on Pearl Harbor hit the radio waves. As people listened to the devastating news, a sense of patriotism and determination swept across the country. Much of the nation's lingering isolationism was quickly extinguished. The following day, President Franklin Delano Roosevelt addressed Congress and urged it to declare war.

> *Yesterday, December 7, 1941—a date which will live in infamy—the United States of America was suddenly and deliberately attacked by naval and air forces of the Empire of Japan. . . . I ask that Congress declare that since the unprovoked and dastardly attack by Japan on Sunday, December 7, 1941, a state of War has existed between the United States and the Japanese Empire.*[13]

Within one hour of Roosevelt's six-minute speech, Congress declared war with a unanimous vote by the Senate and a vote of 388 to 1 in the House of Representatives. The United States of America had officially entered World War II.

2

TURMOIL ABROAD

B y the early 1900s, Japan was a powerful country with a modern navy and a strong army. The country had made industrial and technological advances, expanding its telegraph lines and railroads. Japan's economy had benefited during World War I (1914–1918), when several of the world's strong trading countries endured a war that left Japan relatively unharmed. However, when the worldwide economic downturn known as the Great Depression hit in 1929, Japan was affected by the tumultuous world economic situation.

Japan had set its sights on becoming the most powerful nation in Asia and chose this time to strike. In 1931, the Japanese military invaded Manchuria, a territory now located in northeast China, without the consent of the Japanese government. When Prime Minster Inukai Tsuyoshi objected, the military assassinated him. Throughout the 1930s, Japan fell more and more under military control.

The Japanese invasion devastated Chinese cities in Manchuria.

THE SINO-JAPANESE WAR

In 1937, Japan began a campaign to take over China, launching a full-scale invasion, marching into cities, and killing men, women, and children. By the end of 1938, Japan had extended its control beyond Manchuria into eastern China. The Japanese also occupied Southeast Asia in September 1940 to access the region's natural resources. Japan's aggression brought an outcry from other nations. The United States imposed an embargo on exported goods to Japan, including oil. Without US oil and other resources, Japan would not be able to fuel its continued expansion.

In September 1940, Japan entered into an agreement with Germany and Italy called the Tripartite Pact. The three nations became known as the Axis Powers. They pledged to work together to achieve their military and economic goals. Germany's leader, Adolf Hitler, had set his sights on leading Germany to become the most powerful European nation. His troops invaded Poland, Norway, France, and other countries, and they mounted an aerial attack against the United Kingdom. As war swept through Europe and Asia, the United States was reluctant to involve itself.

German and Japanese officials celebrate the signing of the agreement between their two countries.

Before the attack on Pearl Harbor, a national debate raged in the United States between the interventionists and the isolationists. The interventionists believed the security of the United States depended on the defeat of Germany. They advocated providing aid to the Allies to bring about this defeat. The isolationists believed aid to the Allies would inevitably take the United States down a path to war. They formed the America First Committee to advocate for US neutrality. In early December 1941, polls showed most Americans preferred to stay out of the war. The debate ended in dramatic fashion on the

THE THIRD REICH

The Nazis called the new regime under Hitler the Third Reich, or Third Empire. In their minds, the first empire had been the Holy Roman Empire (962–1806), and the second had lasted from the creation of Germany as a unified nation in 1871 to the end of World War I. During the reign of Kaiser Wilhelm II, who led Germany during the war, the nation became the most powerful country in continental Europe.

chancellor by President Paul von Hindenburg on January 30, 1933. When Hindenburg died of lung cancer in 1934, Hitler combined the positions of chancellor and president and became the absolute dictator of Germany. Hitler became known as the Führer, or leader. The Nazis called the new regime the Third Reich.

Although Hitler had already set secret plans in motion to rebuild Germany's military, he began openly disobeying the Treaty of Versailles and assembling a massive army. He was a powerful, rousing speaker, able to rally Germans around his cause. Hitler believed Germans were the world's master race, and that lower class people were to blame for many of the country's problems. Among these people he included Jews, Slavs, homosexuals, Communists, Roma, and other minorities.

FASCISM IN ITALY AND SPAIN

While Germany dealt with the aftermath of World War I, the next war began brewing elsewhere in Europe. Benito Mussolini, a Fascist military leader, had come to power in Italy in 1922. Like Hitler, Mussolini promised to restore his country to world leadership. He pledged to create an Italian empire around the Mediterranean Sea and began by rebuilding the Italian military.

In October 1935, Mussolini accused Ethiopia of a border violation against one of Italy's African colonies and invaded. As Mussolini's air force bombed villages in Ethiopia, Emperor Haile Selassie sought help from the League of Nations. But while Ethiopians tried in vain to defend themselves with outdated weapons against Italy's tanks, planes, and poison gas, the rest of the world did nothing.

In 1936, civil war broke out in Spain after Spanish troops staged an uprising in Morocco. Spanish general Francisco Franco, also a Fascist, promised his people economic prosperity and political stability. He and his followers, called the Nationalists, waged war against the government of Spain, known as the Republicans.

Mussolini made Ethiopia one of the first nations to fall victim to Europe's Fascist regimes.

Hitler and Mussolini aided Franco. Both supplied tanks, warplanes, and even troops to the Nationalists. Spain would remain officially neutral through World War II. But in the fall of 1936, Italy and Germany signed an alliance, creating the Rome-Berlin Axis.

ISOLATIONISM

The United States stayed out of the Spanish Civil War (1936–1939), though some Americans did volunteer to fight for the Republicans. However, the US government took steps to cut off arms shipments to both sides. In the late 1930s, President Franklin D. Roosevelt signed neutrality acts that made it difficult for the United States to enter into war. Some of these acts forbade US companies from selling weapons to countries at war. Roosevelt used a loophole to get around this restriction regarding China, refusing to acknowledge the country was at war with Japan.

The US government also warned its citizens that those who traveled on passenger ships owned by warring countries did so at their own risk. The United States would not take action on behalf of any citizens harmed on these foreign vessels. One factor that had helped pull the United States into World War I was the sinking of passenger vessels transporting Americans. The government attempted to prevent such an event from drawing it into war again.

THE OUTBREAK OF WAR

Hitler took advantage of the continuing Spanish Civil War to perfect his weaponry and technologies. German planes bombed Republican strongholds, which allowed German pilots to test new techniques and strategies. These developments would lead to the German concept of blitzkrieg, or lightning war. A blitzkrieg used massive aircraft and tank forces to quickly overwhelm an enemy. Some historians view the Spanish Civil War as a practice run for Hitler and his military.

HITLER'S AGGRESSION

In March 1938, Hitler once again ignored the Treaty of Versailles when he sent troops into Austria and united the country with Germany in a nearly bloodless two-day battle.

German and Italian planes bombed the Spanish city of Guernica in April 1937, aiding Franco and practicing their bombardment skills.

Hitler's blitzkrieg tactics used a combination of tanks and ground troops to rapidly conquer territory.

struggle was hopeless. Poland fell within weeks. France and the United Kingdom declared war on Germany on September 3; their endeavors to avoid another world war had been in vain.

As part of the pact with Germany, Stalin quickly invaded Lithuania, Latvia, and Estonia. On November 30, the Soviet Union's armed forces, known as the Red Army, invaded Finland. Stalin wanted to regain some parts of Finland that had once been part of Russia in order to help fortify the Soviet borders.

What he thought would
be another easy conquest
proved to be a ferocious
battle. Though Finland
surrendered after four
months of fighting, the Red
Army took massive losses,
suffering nearly triple the
casualties of Finland's
military.[2]

BLITZKRIEG

Hitler planned to set his
sights on France and the
United Kingdom next. But first, he wanted to secure his
northern flank by capturing seaports in Norway. This would
give the German navy a prime location from which to fight the
British. Although the United Kingdom and France sent aid to
Norway, it did not arrive in time. Germany invaded Norway
and Denmark on April 9, 1940. Both surrendered within a few
months. During the conquest of Norway and Denmark, the
people of the United Kingdom lost confidence in Prime Minister
Neville Chamberlain. It was becoming clear his strategy of

FIGHTING ON SKIS

Stalin had assumed conquering Finland would be
easy. However, his Red Army was not prepared
for the tenacity of the Finnish fighters or their
agility in the snow. During the wintertime war
in 1939, Finnish ski troops easily crossed the
forested, rural terrain of their home country and
contributed greatly to the successes against
the advancing Russian troops. Some Norwegian
troops also fought and traveled on skis as well
as sleds.

appeasement had failed. He was replaced as prime minister by Winston Churchill, who had long warned about Hitler's desire for conquest.

Following the Polish invasion, Hitler increased the production of heavier tanks that were better armored. He ensured Germany would be well armed when it initiated its attacks on Belgium, Luxembourg, and the Netherlands. On May 10, 1940, Germany unleashed blitzkrieg on Western Europe.

When Nazi troops attacked Western Europe on May 10, the Netherlands fell in days. Assault troops landed inside Belgium in gliders. Meanwhile, German forces broke across the Dutch border and headed for Rotterdam, a major city in the Netherlands. French and British forces responded by moving armored divisions north into Belgium to stop the Germans. However, more German troops were making their way north of the French defensive fortifications known as the Maginot Line and through the dense Ardennes Forest. The French had not considered this possibility, believing the forest would serve as a barrier to the German tanks. German general Karl Rudolf Gerd von Rundstedt led his armies through this lightly

Fortifications on the Maginot Line featured concrete bunkers and vast fields of barbed wire.

defended spot. His 7th Panzer Division, led by General Erwin Rommel, emerged from the Ardennes and charged into British troops on the Belgian border. The Germans were stopped briefly at the Meuse River on May 13, but quickly constructed bridges allowing the tanks to cross and continue on. France's Colonel Charles de Gaulle put up a brief counterattack near Montcornet, but his small force was no match for the overwhelming German military.

On May 15, Amsterdam, Holland, fell to Hitler. Less than a week later, German tanks successfully moved across France to reach the English Channel, the body of water separating the islands of the United Kingdom from mainland Europe. Rundstedt's armies trapped hundreds of thousands of British and French troops at the French coastal town of Dunkirk. British naval vessels, accompanied by hundreds of civilian boats, set out across the channel. Under heavy gunfire and constant air attacks, soldiers swam out to meet their rescuers. By the time Dunkirk succumbed to the Germans on June 5, more than 338,000 British and French soldiers had been evacuated back to England.[3]

Rundstedt turned his attention to the South of France. German general Heinz Guderian's tank forces broke through French lines. The Marshal of France, Philippe Pétain, surrendered his country to Germany on June 22. Germany occupied northern France and allowed Pétain to oversee a German-controlled government in the South of France. Many refused to acknowledge the rule of the Germans in the north and Pétain in the south. Some French people joined groups of resistance fighters. De Gaulle fled to London, where he organized a French government-in-exile and joined forces with the United Kingdom. With little effort and few losses, Hitler had conquered Western Europe in less than two months. He then turned his focus to the United Kingdom.

"For days and nights, ships of all kinds have plied to and fro across the channel under the fierce onslaught of the enemy's bombers, utterly regardless of the perils to bring out as many as possible of the trapped BEF [British Expeditionary Force]. There was every kind of ship that I saw coming in this morning. And every one of them was crammed full of tired, battle-stained and bloodstained British soldiers."[4]

—Bernard Stubbs, British radio reporter, May 31, 1940

HALTING THE NAZI ADVANCE

With France and the rest of Western Europe defeated, Hitler made it his goal to conquer the United Kingdom. He planned to put his *Luftwaffe*, or air force, to work attacking the island nation across the English Channel. Prime Minister Churchill prepared his countrymen and women for the German attack. In an address to the British House of Commons in 1940, he promised:

> *We shall not flag or fail. We shall go on to the end. We shall fight in France, we shall fight on the seas and oceans, we shall fight with growing confidence and growing strength in the air. We shall defend our island, whatever the cost may be. We shall fight on the beaches. We shall fight on the landing grounds. We shall fight in*

A German He 111 bomber heads for the United Kingdom in November 1940. The German bombing campaign would seriously test the resolve of the British people.

the fields, and in the streets, we shall fight in the hills. We shall never surrender.[1]

While some British politicians felt it wiser to negotiate with Hitler, Churchill rallied his people and prepared for battle.

THE BLITZ

The Royal Air Force (RAF) Fighter Command of the United Kingdom had sustained heavy losses during the Battle of France, losing about half its planes and pilots. But reinforcements came from Australia, Canada, New Zealand, Poland, South Africa, and other countries.

Hitler prepared an invasion of southern England called Operation Sea Lion. But he knew the still-powerful RAF and Royal Navy would quickly crush any invasion force. Hitler decided he had to clear the RAF from the sky before sending his military across the English Channel. On July 10, 1940, the Luftwaffe began a struggle for the skies over England in what became known as the Battle of Britain.

Throughout the summer of 1940, the Luftwaffe pounded RAF airfields in the United Kingdom. Taking off from northern France, the German Messerschmitt Bf-109 fighter planes had the disadvantage of only holding enough fuel to fight for 15 minutes over England before needing to turn back. The RAF was able to shoot down twice as many German planes as they lost themselves. Thanks to the maneuverability of the Spitfire fighter plane, British pilots had an advantage over their Luftwaffe counterparts flying the Bf-109.

By summer's end, Hermann Göring, head of the Luftwaffe, switched tactics. Instead of bombing airfields during the day, his pilots began bombing cities during the night. Beginning on September 7, London was bombed for 57 nights in a row.[2] Air raid sirens alerted civilians to rush to shelter as German bombs fell on British cities. Many scrambled to London's subway system, the London Underground, for protection. There, they waited as the Blitz continued in the

EVACUATION

During the bombing of the United Kingdom, the British evacuated millions of children from cities under threat of Luftwaffe bombers. Children were placed on trains, often after being split up from siblings and classmates, and sent all over the country to secret destinations to live with strangers in rural areas where it was thought they would be safer. They were given a postcard to send home to their parents, notifying them where they were now living. Some children were not reunited with their families for up to five years.

HITLER ATTACKS RUSSIA

As the United States joined the Allies, Nazi Germany was still holding to its nonaggression pact with the Soviet Union. This would soon end. Hitler hated the Soviet Union and viewed it as being home to Communists and Jews. He planned to invade the enormous country, enslave its people, and take advantage of its natural resources. This move would expand the war dramatically, opening up a second front. Hitler would face off against the British to the West and the Soviets to the East. Some of Hitler's generals feared an attack on the Soviet Union would sap the strength of the German military, but Hitler dismissed their concerns. The quick blitzkrieg victories in Western Europe convinced him it could be done. He argued the United Kingdom would soon fall and the Soviet Union could be taken in a matter of months.

On June 22, 1941, the German invasion of the Soviet Union, called Operation Barbarossa, commenced. Though Stalin was as wary of Hitler as the German leader was of him, he did not expect the Nazis to break their nonaggression pact so soon. Soviet spies had warned him of a buildup of German forces, but Stalin failed to organize a defense. Approximately 3 million German troops marched over the border across a 1,800-mile (2,900 km) front, slamming into the Soviet Union

German troops use a flamethrower to clear a Soviet bunker.

with three army groups: North, South, and Center.[4] The
Luftwaffe destroyed the majority of the Russian air force before
the planes could even become airborne. The Red Army was
unprepared and poorly equipped to defend the Soviet Union.
The Germans made dramatic advances in the first few days,
killing or capturing thousands of Soviet troops.

The Germans pushed farther into the Soviet Union as
the Red Army retreated. By June 27, the Soviet city of Minsk

THE ATLANTIC CHARTER

While Germany and the Soviet Union clashed in the summer of 1941, the United States and the United Kingdom began drawing up plans for the postwar world. In August, Roosevelt and Churchill signed the Atlantic Charter. The document set out several goals. Among them were that the United States and United Kingdom would not seek additional territory as a result of the war, and that any other territorial adjustments around the world would only be made according to the wishes of the people living there. It also called for increased cooperation between nations and the disarmament of the warring countries following the end of the conflict.

had fallen. Hitler's generals desired to press on to Moscow, the Soviet Union's capital. But Hitler transferred two of his tank units from the Center group to the other two groups in the north and south. The North and South groups were marching toward the city of Leningrad and Ukraine, respectively, while the Center group was aiming for Moscow. As a result of the transfer, the Center group slowed and gave Stalin time to reinforce Moscow.

By September 19, German troops took the city of Kiev, Ukraine, capturing some 665,000 Soviet soldiers. By this time, the Soviet death toll had reached 700,000, with another 1.5 million taken as prisoners of war.[5] Hitler now turned his attention to capturing Moscow. But the autumn brought miserable rains that turned roads to mud and made transport incredibly difficult. Supplies began to run out and temperatures fell. German soldiers were not prepared with cold-weather clothing, and their losses were much more severe than in the Western European campaigns. By the end of November, they had suffered 730,000 casualties.[6]

Russian civilians joined in the war effort to dig trenches and defend Moscow. Winter brought howling winds, snow, and temperatures that plunged to -40 degrees Fahrenheit (-40°C).[7] Weapons failed to fire in the biting temperatures, and tanks once stuck in the mud were now frozen in the earth. Just miles from Moscow, the Germans were forced to fall back in the face of a Soviet counteroffensive on December 6. Hitler's mighty army had its first taste of defeat.

5

THE UNITED STATES ENTERS THE WAR

With mainland Europe quickly becoming an impenetrable fortress, the United Kingdom took the fight against the Axis to North Africa. Coming from Egypt, British troops had crossed much of Libya in early 1941 and destroyed Mussolini's Italian forces there. Because Hitler could not let North Africa fall to the British, he sent reinforcements known as the Afrika Korps. The widely respected general Erwin Rommel led this tank division. Rommel's tactics were so clever, he earned the nickname "The Desert Fox" from the British. The Germans and British fought back-and-forth battles in the desert. Though thousands were killed on both sides, victory proved elusive.

British troops run for cover after placing an explosive charge on a German tank in North Africa.

DOOLITTLE RAID

On April 18, 1942, Lieutenant Colonel James "Jimmy" Doolittle led the first air raid on the Japanese home islands. Just months after Pearl Harbor, and with the Japanese still advancing through the Pacific Ocean, the raid was intended to boost US morale and cause the Japanese people to doubt their own leadership. Sixteen B-25B Mitchell bombers were launched from the aircraft carrier *Hornet* in the West Pacific. Each plane was to bomb military targets in Japan and then continue on to China, where they would land. The planes successfully hit some of their targets, but none managed to land in China. The crews were forced to parachute out or crash-land. A total of 11 crewmen were killed or captured.[2]

in May and June. At Midway, Nimitz's carrier-based warplanes sank four Japanese aircraft carriers. The battle marked the end of Japanese expansion. The tide had turned in the Pacific war.

In August, US troops gained beachheads on Guadalcanal, one of the Solomon Islands off the northeast coast of Australia. Taking Guadalcanal would ensure that shipping lanes would remain open between the United States and Australia. MacArthur's troops endured harsh jungle conditions and enemies who refused to surrender. The Japanese troops, made to believe surrender was dishonorable, were often ordered to fight to the death. The struggle dragged on for months. Finally, the Japanese evacuated Guadalcanal

US Marines guard a light tank in Guadalcanal's heavy jungle terrain.

in February 1943, having suffered the loss of 24,000 men compared to the United States' 1,600. Thousands more died of tropical diseases, such as malaria.[3]

6

THE TIDE TURNS

In late December 1941, Roosevelt and Churchill met in Washington, DC, to discuss strategies for defeating the Axis. Throughout the war, the two leaders met frequently to discuss strategy. They agreed the United States should send troops to Western Europe, opening up a second front to relieve Stalin's forces in the east. But they disagreed about where and when the invasion of Europe would take place.

Roosevelt finally agreed to Churchill's plan to send troops to North Africa first, although his initial thoughts were to immediately invade northern France and press on to Germany. Churchill believed they should strike Germany where it was most vulnerable.

Rommel and his tank divisions launched a major offensive in April 1941, rolling through Libya and into Egypt. The British forces repelled him in Operation Crusader in November.

Churchill, *left*, and Roosevelt, *right*, give a press conference on December 23, 1941.

THE WAR TOUCHES EVERYONE

One of Hitler's motives for waging war was to eliminate what he considered to be lower classes of people. While this included minorities such as Roma, homosexuals, and people with disabilities, Hitler had an especially intense hatred for Jews. All of these groups were sent to Nazi concentration camps and death camps to be used as slave labor or murdered. The inhabitants of these camps faced perhaps the most brutal and inhumane circumstances of World War II.

Hitler's anti-Semitism stemmed from his blaming of the Jews for the crippling inflation of the 1920s and the depression of the 1930s. He also claimed they were responsible for the

Jewish citizens of Warsaw, the capital of Poland, were removed from their homes at gunpoint.

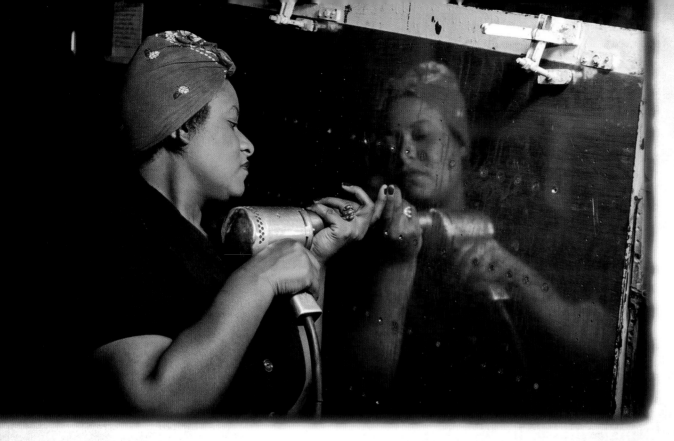

A US worker constructs an A-31 bomber aircraft in February 1943.

ON THE HOME FRONT

Following the Pearl Harbor attack, Roosevelt explained the importance of wartime industry to the American people:

> *Powerful enemies must be out-fought and out-produced.
> It is not enough to turn out just a few more planes, a few
> more tanks, a few more guns. . . . We must out-produce
> them overwhelmingly, so that there can be no question of*

our ability to provide a crushing superiority of equipment
in any theatre of the world war.[2]

Americans answered his call. Throughout the war, no
country matched the United States in war production. Nearly
two-thirds of all Allied military equipment produced for the
war effort was manufactured in the United States, including
297,000 aircraft, 193,000 artillery pieces, 86,000 tanks, and 2
million army trucks.[3] In four years, the United States' industrial
production doubled. The other Allies ramped up their
production as well. In general, the Allied production efforts far
outpaced those of the Axis powers.

With so many men called into military service, US industry
turned to women to find the workers needed to keep plants
and factories churning out weapons, vehicles, and ammunition.
A propaganda campaign used posters and advertisements
to encourage US women to support the war effort by taking
factory jobs. When the United States entered World War II,
12 million women held jobs. By the end of the war, nearly
18 million women were in the workforce.[4] Some worked in
factories and other blue-collar jobs, while many others took
clerical positions.

ROSIE THE RIVETER

When the United States entered World War II, women worked in a variety of positions that formerly were only held by men. More than 310,000 women took jobs in the aircraft industry in 1943, while many others found work in the munitions industry.[6]

A US government propaganda poster showed an illustration of a female assembly line worker wearing a bandana and flexing her bicep. Dubbed Rosie the Riveter, the character soon became an iconic image of US women in the World War II workforce. Rosie served as a reminder to US women that they were important to the war effort and encouraged, "We Can Do It!"[7]

As the war continued, the military had priority over civilians when it came to scarce resources. Nylon and silk were no longer used for clothing, but rather for parachutes and uniforms. Metal, rubber, and leather were needed by the military. Food and items such as shoes, gasoline, and metal were soon controlled by a ration system that limited how much a civilian was allowed to purchase. Governments also ran campaigns to collect and recycle scrap metal to be melted down to make bombs and bullets. During one of these campaigns, 5 million tons of steel were received in just three weeks.[5]

Vegetables were grown wherever possible, from the sides of roads to people's backyards, in what became known as victory gardens. By 1943, 40 percent of fresh vegetables in the United States were grown in these victory gardens.[8] Butter, sugar, and meat were in short supply, so people altered recipes to make the most of what they had.

JAPANESE-AMERICAN INTERNMENT CAMPS

Patriotism surged during the war. Many Europeans had immigrated in the decades before World War II, and most were well established in the United States and trusted by their fellow Americans. But for Japanese Americans in the days and months following the attack at Pearl Harbor, the situation was different. The government and their own neighbors questioned their loyalty, openly wondering whether they were on the side of the United States in the war against Japan. Racism against people of Japanese ancestry fueled these suspicions. At the time, Japanese Americans living on the West Coast numbered more than 120,000.[9] Most were legal US citizens.

Still, people feared Japanese Americans would commit acts of sabotage to hinder the war effort. Roosevelt issued Executive Order 9066, allowing the government to forcefully relocate Japanese Americans to War Relocation Camps in states such as Arizona, Colorado, Wyoming, and Utah. While the camps

STORIES FROM THE WAR

Grace Aiko Obata Amemiya was a Japanese-American woman sent to an internment camp. Years later, she recalled the experience of leaving her old life behind:

"We had to leave our homes, yes, but we had to dispose of everything we had: cars, things in the home, furniture and everything. . . . We were given these baggage tags with this number and we had to wear it on all our garments and everything we carried. In other words, we weren't a family name anymore, we were family 6051. . . . They said the internment was for our protection. And our next question was, we said, 'If so, why were the guns pointed at us instead of outward?'"[10]

A Japanese-American family awaits the bus that will take them to an internment camp.

were a far cry from the concentration camps in Europe, those who were interned lost their homes and jobs. It was not until 1990 that the US government gave reparation payments to the remaining survivors.

A VIOLENT END

Roosevelt, Churchill, and Stalin met in Tehran, Iran, in the closing months of 1943. There, they coordinated their efforts to strike against Germany. It was decided that Churchill and Roosevelt would launch an invasion of Western Europe in mid-1944. This would relieve pressure on Stalin's forces in Eastern Europe.

Meanwhile, in the Pacific Ocean, Nimitz engaged in an island-hopping campaign, conquering island after island on the way to Japan. MacArthur focused on retaking the Philippines. In some cases, they were able to simply neutralize Japanese forces on small islands by heavy bombing, bypassing the area without landing troops. However, landings were sometimes necessary to destroy entrenched Japanese positions, especially on islands holding major value for the war effort. In order to support an assault on the Marianas Islands west of Guadalcanal, US marines would need to take over the tiny

Stalin, *left*, Roosevelt, *center*, and Churchill, *right*, all met together for the first time at the Tehran Conference.

island of Betio, part of the Tarawa Atoll. The landings were set for late November 1943.

The Battle of Tarawa was the first landing in the Pacific Ocean to face immediate heavy resistance. A total of 18,000 marines were sent to take the island, and 4,500 Japanese defenders were in place.[1] After low tides left some landing ships stuck on coral reefs offshore, marines were forced to leave their boats and wade hundreds of yards through the water under heavy fire to reach the beaches. Then, they inched slowly forward, using grenades and flamethrowers to destroy fortified enemy positions. The battle lasted 76 hours. More than 1,000 US troops and all but 17 of the Japanese troops were dead.[2]

OPERATION OVERLORD

In late 1943 and early 1944, Allied forces in Europe geared up to launch Operation Overlord, a massive invasion of Western Europe. Over the course of two years, a huge invasion force assembled in the United Kingdom. Nearly 3 million troops and thousands of naval vessels under Eisenhower's command were prepared to land along the coast of Normandy in France.[3] It was the largest invasion force in history. On the evening of June 5,

The beachhead at Normandy was secured by hundreds of ships and floating barrage balloons. The balloons' metal cables were designed to stop low-flying enemy aircraft.

1944, Eisenhower visited with troops, who assured him they were ready to perform their duties.

The next morning at 6:30 a.m., amphibious landing craft began depositing a first-day total of 160,000 Allied troops onto a 50-mile (80 km) stretch of beaches in Normandy.[4] Five invasion beaches were given names and divided between the Allied forces. Canadian troops would land at Juno beach. The British would take Gold and Sword beaches. And the Americans would seize Utah and Omaha beaches. Despite heavy losses, the Allied forces successfully took their assigned beaches. By the end of the day, fresh Allied troops and equipment streamed

Operation Overlord was the massive invasion of Western Europe by Allied forces through Normandy, France. The invasion itself was preceded by a major disinformation campaign designed to trick the Germans into expecting the attack somewhere else. Fake radio broadcasts suggested the landings would come farther to the east than actually planned. The Germans fell for the deception and moved large portions of their defensive forces to this area.

US troops at Utah beach were confronted with light opposition and captured the landing area relatively easily. However, Omaha beach was defended by a skilled German unit, and the terrain made a direct assault extremely difficult. Defensive positions on high bluffs had clear views of the beach, and only narrow pathways led from the beach to this high ground.

When the loading ramps of the first landing craft dropped, machine gun fire rained down on troops already queasy from the choppy waters. Soldiers scrambled to wade from their landing craft to the beaches. Chaos and confusion reigned as the beaches erupted in fire and explosions. The US forces

US troops wade ashore at Omaha Beach.

suffered 2,400 casualties trying to take the beach.[5] With officers being killed around them, small groups of soldiers formed improvised groups and managed to make their way up the beach. Finally, they reached their objective and established a beachhead.

continuously onto the beaches. By early July, 1 million Allied soldiers stood on French soil.[6] The Allies had successfully taken a foothold in Western Europe.

PUSHING THE GERMANS BACK

From Normandy, the Allies made their way into the heart of France. Troops under US generals Omar Bradley and Patton moved inland. By August 25, Paris was liberated from Nazi occupation. The Germans were pushed out of France and Belgium by mid-September.

In December, German forces launched one last massive offensive through the Ardennes Forest in Belgium and France. In the early morning of December 16, 200,000 German troops and nearly 1,000 tanks crashed through the snow-covered pine trees and surprised US troops stationed there.[7] A barrage of artillery shook the forest while US soldiers huddled in foxholes.

US troops were pushed back 60 miles (100 km) to the Belgian town of Bastogne, creating a huge bulge in the Allied lines.[8] For six days the Americans held out, fighting desperately to hold the town amid the brutal winter conditions. Finally, the skies cleared enough for Allied planes to drop supplies into Bastogne. Bombers attacked German positions, and by

US troops take up a defensive position in the snow during the Battle of the Bulge.

December 26 Bastogne was liberated. The struggle, commonly called the Battle of the Bulge, continued into January until the Germans were finally pushed back. Allied troops began flooding into Germany.

VICTORY IN EUROPE

By April 1945, Soviets coming from the east had reached the outskirts of Berlin. As they entered the city, Hitler sat in his fortified bunker with his top advisors. Knowing his reign as Führer had come to an end, he married his mistress Eva Braun on April 29. The next day, the couple went alone into his

The Battle of Leyte Gulf, fought in late October 1944, was the largest naval battle in world history. Following a US beach assault on the island of Leyte in the Philippines, Japan sent a naval force to attack the landings. The Imperial Japanese Navy had been crippled by its previous encounters with the US Navy and sent its best remaining ships to combat the invasion. Four Japanese naval groups would face off against the US Seventh Fleet and the US Third Fleet.

The Japanese plan was to use one of its naval groups as a decoy to draw the Third Fleet away from the area. Meanwhile, the other three groups would surround and attack the Seventh Fleet, which was supporting the US invasion forces. One would come from the north and two would come from the south. The Third Fleet chased the decoy, but on October 23, US submarines discovered the two attacking naval groups coming from the south. Now aware of the incoming attackers, the Seventh Fleet set up a trap and destroyed nearly all of the ships in one of the groups. The second group coming from the south, seeing the wreckage of the first group, retreated.

More than 200 ships and 1,000 planes were involved in the Battle of Leyte Gulf.

However, the Japanese naval force coming from the north was still approaching through the gap left by the Third Fleet, surprising the Seventh Fleet. The US ships launched waves of carrier aircraft to attack the Japanese forces and give the vulnerable carriers themselves time to escape. In all, US Navy ships and aircraft sank 27 Japanese ships, including four aircraft carriers and three battleships. The US Navy lost only six ships.[9]

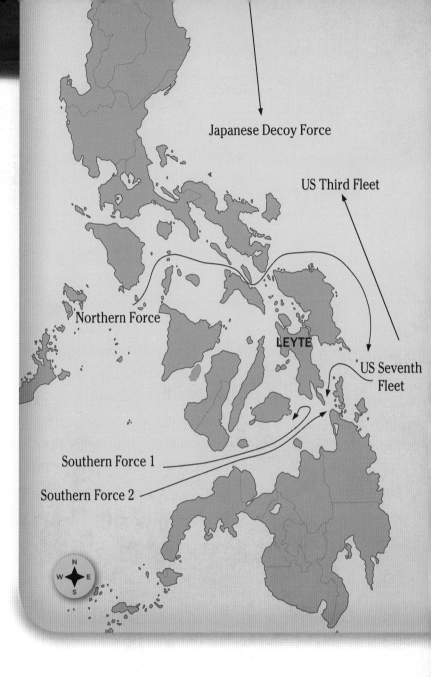

Japanese Decoy Force

US Third Fleet

Northern Force

LEYTE

US Seventh Fleet

Southern Force 1

Southern Force 2

N W E S

Its airfield would make it possible for US fighter planes to defend bombers carrying out missions over Japan. In February 1945, a landing on the island resulted in 6,000 US deaths.[10] Troops finally won control over Iwo Jima in mid-March.

Following the victory was a devastating battle for the Okinawa Islands. The islands, only a few hundred miles from Japan's home islands, would be the final stepping stones to an all-out invasion of Japan. Approximately 75,000 Japanese troops defended the largest island, called Okinawa.[11] On April 1, 60,000 US troops landed, beginning the Battle of Okinawa.[12] The land battle was extremely fierce, with fanatical Japanese soldiers fighting to the death in most cases. In the air, Japanese pilots known as kamikaze pilots flew planes loaded with explosives directly into US ships. By the end of the Okinawa campaign, 12,000 US and 100,000 Japanese soldiers were dead.[16]

THE ATOMIC BOMB FALLS

US military leaders felt an invasion of Japan would result in hundreds of thousands of Allied casualties. Still, the need to achieve an absolute victory over Japan seemed to make an invasion necessary. Plans were drawn up for Operation Downfall, the invasion of the Japanese home islands. The invasion would dwarf even the massive invasion of Normandy in Europe. Estimates suggested more than 200,000 US soldiers would be killed or wounded in Operation Downfall. The total number of casualties for the United States in the Pacific war up to that point was 170,000.[14] Truman, Stalin, and Churchill met in Potsdam, Germany, to decide how to proceed. They served Japan an ultimatum: surrender or face total destruction.

Just before the Potsdam conference, Truman was provided with a new weapon. After four years of research, physicists working with the US military had succeeded in developing the world's first atomic bomb. On July 16, 1945, the

THE MANHATTAN PROJECT

In 1938, physicists discovered how to split an atom, the smallest building block of all matter. Leading scientists knew there was a very good chance the Germans could use this discovery to create a devastating bomb. Physicists Albert Einstein, who had fled Nazi Germany, and Enrico Fermi, who had escaped fascist Italy, both immigrated to the United States. The two successfully convinced Roosevelt of the dangers of this technological advancement. In late 1941, a US effort to build an atomic bomb began. The code name for this extensive top-secret research project was the Manhattan Project. By December 1942, Fermi had succeeded in starting the first controlled nuclear chain reaction. On July 16, 1945, the first nuclear bomb was tested at Alamogordo, New Mexico.

bomb was tested in a remote desert area in New Mexico. The single bomb had the power of approximately 20,000 short tons (18,000 metric tons) of conventional explosives.[15]

When Japan refused to give in, Truman decided to drop an atomic bomb on a Japanese city in an attempt to force them to surrender. He hoped the atomic bomb would make the invasion of Japan unnecessary. On August 6, 1945, a B-29 bomber named the *Enola Gay* dropped an atomic bomb on the Japanese city of Hiroshima. The blast annihilated everything in an area of 4.4 square miles (11.4 sq km) and killed 70,000 people, mostly civilians.[16] Tens of thousands more would later die of radiation poisoning caused by the bomb.

The Japanese still did not surrender. On August 8, the Soviet Union declared war on Japan, fulfilling Stalin's promise to join the war once Germany was defeated. Hours later, masses of Soviet troops invaded Japanese-held Manchuria. The next day, the United States dropped another atomic bomb on the city of Nagasaki, killing approximately 40,000 more Japanese civilians.[17] The emperor of Japan announced his nation's surrender on August 10. The Allies accepted the terms of surrender on August 14. Three weeks later, on September 2, the Japanese signed surrender documents in Tokyo Bay aboard the *Missouri,* a battleship that had seen action at Iwo Jima and

An atomic bomb turned many of the buildings and people of Hiroshima to dust.

Okinawa. VJ Day, or Victory over Japan Day, was celebrated throughout the United States. World War II was finally over.

LEAVING
U.S. SECTOR
BERLIN
YOU ARE NOW
ENTERING
BRITISH SECTOR
Sailer
53

9

AFTERMATH

While the Allies celebrated the long-awaited end of World War II, people in the war-torn regions of the world struggled to put their lives back together. Massive loss of life and the destruction of homes, neighborhoods, and whole cities left millions wondering what to do next.

Stalin acknowledged, "It is not so difficult to keep unity in time of war, since there is a joint aim to defeat the common enemy, which is clear to everyone. The difficult time will come after the war, when diverse interests tend to divide the allies."[1] The time had come to deal with the aftermath of war.

A CONTINENT IN RUIN

One of the most horrific discoveries Allied troops made was the condition of victims of Nazi concentration camps. Prisoners were so emaciated they seemed to be nothing

German women begin the process of clearing rubble from their ruined cities.

Following the war, Allied troops continued to occupy Germany and Japan for several years as the two nations transitioned from war to peacetime. The United States wrote a new constitution for Japan, modeling it after the US Constitution. The Allied occupation of Japan ended in 1951, though thousands of US troops remain on military bases there. In Japan, the occupation government included many Japanese leaders. But in Germany, the Allies ran a military government until 1949.

RELIEF EFFORTS

Beginning as early as 1942, the Allies realized the need to provide relief to countries liberated from Axis control. Twenty-six nations came together to form a group called the United Nations. One of their first tasks was to form the United Nations Relief and Rehabilitation Administration. Under this organization, they sent livestock and food to war-torn Europe. The Marshall Plan, established in 1948, was a US program designed to provide aid to Western Europe. The plan also aimed to prevent communism from taking hold in the devastated regions. Despite this assistance, the effects of the war would linger for years as Europeans struggled to cobble their lives back together.

Other Allied postwar programs sought to punish Nazi war criminals. Under these programs, the world was exposed to the inhumane behavior of Axis leaders. These men were put on trial for war crimes in the German city of Nuremberg in 1945. After extensive investigations and trials, 12 Nazi leaders were sentenced to death and eight were given life in prison. Another 77 were given shorter sentences. The remaining 86 were acquitted of their charges.[3] Similar war crime tribunals were held in Tokyo, and seven were sentenced to death.

THE IRON CURTAIN DESCENDS

Although the United States and the United Kingdom had allied with the Soviet Union to win the war, they did not share its political ideology. After World War II, a tense struggle began between Communist and non-Communist powers. The Soviet Union had already imposed a Communist government in Poland, which would last until 1989. Part of the Soviet Union's bitterness toward its allies stemmed from the fact that it suffered the vast majority of Allied casualties during the war. Approximately 11 million Soviet soldiers and 7 million Soviet civilians had been killed between 1941 and 1945.[4] By comparison, the United States and the United Kingdom had each lost fewer than 300,000 soldiers.[5]

East Germany fell under Communist Soviet rule, as did Hungary, Bulgaria, and eventually Czechoslovakia. The Soviet Union and the United States found themselves in a cold war. There was no direct conflict between them, but each sought to maintain and extend its influence across the world. Stalin believed the United States was on a crusade to put an end to communism. Informed by his spies of the atomic bomb program before even Truman knew, Stalin set his scientists to work developing a bomb of their own. The United States responded by developing ever more powerful weaponry. The back-and-forth contest to build more destructive weapons was known as the arms race. It was a battle that would extend into the 1980s.

POSTWAR UNITED STATES

The United States emerged from World War II with unprecedented industrial might. In five years, the nation had turned into a powerhouse of agriculture and industry. Factories reverted from producing planes and tanks to producing peacetime goods.

Men returned from fighting overseas and resumed positions in the workforce. While some women remained

The US economy rapidly shifted production from war products to a vast array of consumer goods, such as electric washing machines.

working, many employers forced them into lower-paying jobs or out of their jobs entirely. Many returned to being homemakers. Yet they had blazed a trail for future generations of women in the workplace.

The United States had not fought in World War II from the conflict's beginning. But after being drawn in by the attack on Pearl Harbor, the nation and its people set out to end it. From the victory gardens on the home front to the naval battles of the Pacific Ocean to the storming of Normandy, the United States made significant and decisive contributions to the Allied war effort.

1939

On September 1, Hitler's army invades Poland.

1939

On September 3, France and the United Kingdom declare war on Germany.

1941

On December 7, Japan attacks Pearl Harbor.

1941

On December 8, the United States and the United Kingdom declare war on Japan.

1942

On June 4, the United States defeats Japan at the Battle of Midway.

1944

Allied troops land at Normandy, France, on June 6.

1944

US and French troops liberate Paris on August 25.

1945

Adolf Hitler commits suicide on April 30.

1945

Germany stops fighting and surrenders on May 7.

1945

The United States drops an atomic bomb on Hiroshima, Japan, on August 6.

1945

On August 9, another atomic bomb is dropped on Nagasaki, Japan.

1945

Japan surrenders and the Allies accept the terms on August 14.

1945

Japan signs surrender documents in Tokyo Bay on September 2.

WORLD WAR II BATTLES IN THE PACIFIC, 1941–1945

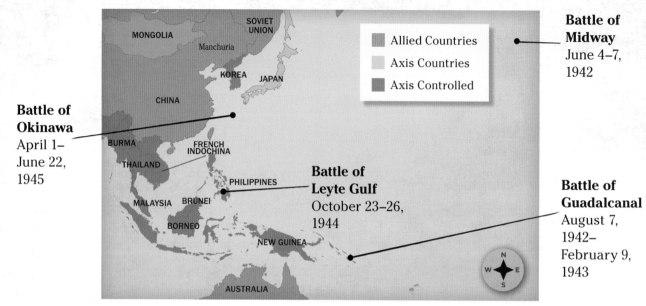

Battle of Midway
June 4–7, 1942

Battle of Okinawa
April 1–
June 22,
1945

Battle of Leyte Gulf
October 23–26,
1944

Battle of Guadalcanal
August 7,
1942–
February 9,
1943

Allied Countries
Axis Countries
Axis Controlled

CASUALTIES

Total American Casualties: 1,076,245

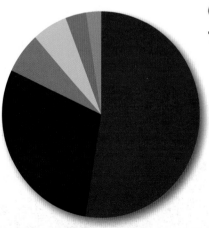

- Army deaths: 318,274
- Navy deaths: 62,614
- Marines deaths: 24,511
- Army wounded: 565,861
- Navy wounded: 37,778
- Marines wounded: 67,207

Battle of the Bulge
December 16, 1944–January 25, 1945

Operation Overlord
June 6–August 25, 1944

Operation Torch
November 8–16, 1942

Legend:
- Allied Countries
- Axis Countries
- Axis Controlled
- Neutral

KEY PLAYERS

Adolf Hitler was the leader of Nazi Germany.

Franklin Delano Roosevelt was president of the United States during World War II.

Joseph Stalin was the leader of the Soviet Union.

Winston Churchill was the prime minister of the United Kingdom.

armistice

A truce or temporary peace agreement.

artillery

Large weapons used to fire long-range explosives.

beachhead

A position on a beach that can be defended.

blitzkrieg

A war using a forceful, violent, and quick offensive.

convoy

A protective escort.

dictator

A leader who has complete control over a country.

embargo

An order by a government prohibiting trade and commerce with another country.

fascism

A political theory that places the importance of the nation above that of the individual.

interventionism

A policy of supporting government interference in economic or political affairs of another country.

isolationism

A national policy of abstaining from becoming involved in other countries' political and economic affairs.

occupy

To take possession of or take control over.

propaganda

Ideas or information spread to further a cause.

refugee

A person who flees home to escape danger.

regime

A government's period of rule over a country.

shrapnel

Bomb or shell fragments resulting from an explosion.

SELECTED BIBLIOGRAPHY

Hastings, Max. *Inferno: The World at War, 1939–1945*. New York: Vintage, 2011. Print.

FURTHER READINGS

Gitlin, Martin. *George S. Patton: World War II General & Military Innovator (Military Heroes)*. Minneapolis, MN: ABDO, 2010. Print.

World War II: The Definitive Visual History. New York: DK, 2011. Print.

WEB SITES

To learn more about World War II, visit ABDO Publishing Company online at **www.abdopublishing.com**. Web sites about World War II are featured on our Book Links page. These links are routinely monitored and updated to provide the most current information available.

PLACES TO VISIT

National Museum of the United States Air Force
1100 Spaatz Street
Wright-Patterson AFB, OH 45433
937-255-3286
http://www.nationalmuseum.af.mil
This enormous museum features military airplanes from every era of US military aviation. Included among the exhibits is the actual B-29 bomber that dropped an atomic bomb on Nagasaki.

The National World War II Museum
945 Magazine Street
New Orleans, LA 70130
504-528-1944
http://www.ddaymuseum.org
The National World War II Museum features exhibits and artifacts from both the European and Pacific theatres of the war.

CHAPTER 1. DAY OF INFAMY

1. Megan Gambino. "Unflinching Portraits of Pearl Harbor Survivors." *Smithsonian. com*. Smithsonian Media, 5 Dec. 2011. Web. 16 Apr. 2013.

2. "The Attack on Pearl Harbor." *Remembering Pearl Harbor: The USS Arizona Memorial*. National Park Service, n.d. Web. 16 Apr. 2013.

3. Walter Lord. *Day of Infamy*. New York: Holt, 1985. Print. 44.

4. Ibid. 45.

5. Ibid. 109.

6. "Honoring the Oklahoma." *USS Oklahoma Memorial*. National Park Service, n.d. Web. 17 Apr. 2013.

7. "History and Culture." *World War II Valor in the Pacific*. National Park Service, 24 Mar. 2013. Web. 17 Apr. 2013.

8. "Pearl Harbor Casualties." *PearlHarbor.org*. PearlHarbor.org, 2013. Web. 17 Apr. 2013.

9. "Fact Sheet: Pearl Harbor." *US Navy Museum*. US Navy, n.d. Web. 17 Apr. 2013.

10. "Pearl Harbor Casualties." *PearlHarbor.org*. PearlHarbor.org, 2013. Web. 17 Apr. 2013.

11. "Pearl Harbor Attack." *Encyclopaedia Britannica*. Encyclopaedia Britannica, 2013. Web. 17 Apr. 2013.

12. Allan Kent Powell. "Utahn Survives the Attack on Pearl Harbor." *Utah History to Go*. State of Utah, Mar. 1996. Web. 17 Apr. 2013.

13. Franklin Delano Roosevelt. "'Day of Infamy' Speech: Joint Address to Congress Leading to a Declaration of War against Japan." *America's Historical Documents*. National Archives, 2013. Web. 17 Apr. 2013.

CHAPTER 2. TURMOIL ABROAD

None.

CHAPTER 3. THE OUTBREAK OF WAR

1. "World War II." *Encyclopaedia Britannica*. Encyclopaedia Britannica, 2013. Web. 17 Apr. 2013.

2. Ibid.

3. "Dunkirk Evacuation." *Encyclopaedia Britannica*. Encyclopaedia Britannica, 2013. Web. 17 Apr. 2013.

4. "Dunkirk Evacuation." *BBC Archive*. BBC, 2013. Web. 17 Apr. 2013.

CHAPTER 4. HALTING THE NAZI ADVANCE

1. "'We Shall Fight on the Beaches,' 4 June 1940." *Audio: Churchill and World War II*. BBC, 2013. Web. 17 Apr. 2013.

2. "Battle of Britain." *Encyclopaedia Britannica*. Encyclopaedia Britannica, 2013. Web. 17 Apr. 2013.

3. "Arsenal of Democracy." *Encyclopedia of Detroit*. Detroit Historical Society, 2013. Web. 17 Apr. 2013.

4. "Operation Barbarossa." *Encyclopaedia Britannica*. Encyclopaedia Britannica, 2013. Web. 17 Apr. 2013.

5. James L. Stokesbury. "World War II." *World Book Advanced*. World Book, 2013. Web. 3 Jan. 2013.

6. "Operation Barbarossa." *Encyclopaedia Britannica*. Encyclopaedia Britannica, 2013. Web. 17 Apr. 2013.

7. Erik Sass. "Operation Barbarossa: The Largest Military Adventure in History." *Mental Floss*. Mental Floss, 21 June 2011. Web. 18 Apr. 2013.

CHAPTER 5. THE UNITED STATES ENTERS THE WAR

1. "Bataan Death March." *Encyclopaedia Britannica*. Encyclopaedia Britannica, 2013. Web. 17 Apr. 2013.

2. "The Doolittle Raid." *WWII Combat*. USS Hornet Museum, 2008. Web. 18 Apr. 2013.

3. "Battle of Guadalcanal." *Encyclopaedia Britannica*. Encyclopaedia Britannica, 2013. Web. 17 Apr. 2013.

CHAPTER 6. THE TIDE TURNS

1. "World War II." *Encyclopaedia Britannica*. Encyclopaedia Britannica, 2013. Web. 17 Apr. 2013.

2. "Battle of the Kasserine Pass." *This Day in History*. History Channel, 2013. Web. 18 Apr. 2013.

3. "World War II." *Encyclopaedia Britannica*. Encyclopaedia Britannica, 2013. Web. 17 Apr. 2013.

4. "Italian Campaign." *History Channel*. History Channel, 2013. Web. 18 Apr. 2013.

5. Donald L. Miller. *The Story of World War II*. New York: Simon, 2001. Print. 216.

CHAPTER 7. THE WAR TOUCHES EVERYONE

1. Michael Berenbaum. "Holocaust." *World Book Advanced*. World Book, 2013. Web. 18 Apr. 2013.

2. "War Production." *The War*. PBS, 2007. Web. 18 Apr. 2013.

3. Ibid.

4. "Rosie the Riveter: Women Working During World War II." *National Park Service*. National Park Service, n.d. Web. 18 Apr. 2013.

5. Cecil Adams. "Were WWII Scrap Drives Just a Ploy to Boost Morale?" *Straight Dope*. Sun-Times Media, 2013. Web. 4 Apr. 2013.

6. "Rosie the Riveter." *History Channel*. History Channel, 2013. Web. 18 Apr. 2013.

7. Ibid.

8. Cecil Adams. "Were WWII Scrap Drives Just a Ploy to Boost Morale?" *Straight Dope*. Sun-Times Media, 2013. Web. 4 Apr. 2013.

9. "Internment History." *Children of the Camps*. PBS, 1999. Web. 18 Apr. 2013.

10. Katherine Klingseis. "Amemiya Shares Stories of Living in Internment Camps, Urges People to 'Keep a Positive Attitude.'" *Iowa State Daily*. Iowa State Daily, 3 Mar. 2012. Web. 18 Apr. 2013.

CHAPTER 8. A VIOLENT END

1. "Battle of Tarawa." *History Channel*. History Channel, 2013. Web. 18 Apr. 2013.

2. Ibid.

3. "Animated Map: Operation Overlord." *History*. BBC, n.d. Web. 18 Apr. 2013.

4. "D-Day." *US Army*. US Army, n.d. Web. 18 Apr. 2013.

5. "Omaha Beach." *Encyclopaedia Britannica*. Encyclopaedia Britannica, 2013. Web. 17 Apr. 2013.

6. Bruce W. Nelan. "D-Day." *Time*. Time, 24 June 2001. Web. 18 Apr. 2013.

7. "The Battle of the Bulge." *US Army*. US Army, n.d. Web. 18 Apr. 2013.

8. "Battle of the Bulge Begins." *This Day in History*. History Channel, 2013. Web. 18 Apr. 2013.

9. Kennedy Hickman. "World War II: Battle of Leyte Gulf." *About.com*. About.com, 2013. Web. 18 Apr. 2013.

10. "World War II." *Encyclopaedia Britannica*. Encyclopaedia Britannica, 2013. Web. 17 Apr. 2013.

11. Ibid.

12. Ibid.

13. Ibid.

14. "The Decision to Use the Atomic Bomb." *Encyclopaedia Britannica*. Encyclopaedia Britannica, 2013. Web. 17 Apr. 2013.

15. "The Manhattan Project." *Encyclopaedia Britannica*. Encyclopaedia Britannica, 2013. Web. 17 Apr. 2013.

16. "The Decision to Use the Atomic Bomb." *Encyclopaedia Britannica*. Encyclopaedia Britannica, 2013. Web. 17 Apr. 2013.

17. Ibid.

CHAPTER 9. AFTERMATH

1. C. L. Sulzberger. *World War II*. New York: Houghton, 1967. Print. 133.

2. "Liberation of Nazi Camps." *Holocaust Encyclopedia*. United States Holocaust Memorial Museum, 11 May 2012. Web. 19 Apr. 2013.

3. "Subsequent Nuremberg Proceedings." *Holocaust Encyclopedia*. United States Holocaust Memorial Museum, 11 May 2012. Web. 19 Apr. 2013.

4. "World War II." *Encyclopaedia Britannica*. Encyclopaedia Britannica, 2013. Web. 17 Apr. 2013.

5. Ibid.

Japan, 7–8, 17, 19–20, 27, 50–53, 54, 71, 75, 82–83, 84, 86–89, 94
Japanese-American internment, 71–73

Kasserine Pass, Battle of the, 58–59

League of Nations, 22, 25
Lend-Lease Act, 43
Leyte Gulf, Battle of, 84–85
London, United Kingdom, 37, 41
Luftwaffe, 39–42, 45, 82

MacArthur, Douglas, 53–54, 75, 82
Maginot Line, 34
Manchuria, 19–20, 88
Marshall Plan, 94
Midway, Battle of, 53–54
Moscow, Soviet Union, 46–47, 50
Munich Agreement, 30

Mussolini, Benito, 25–26, 49, 60–61

Nagasaki, Japan, 88
Nazi Party, 23–24, 65–66
Nimitz, Chester, 53–54, 75
Normandy, France, 76–77, 78–79, 80, 87
Nuremberg Trials, 94–95

occupations, 94
oil, 8, 20, 43, 59
Okinawa, Battle of, 86, 89
Operation Barbarossa, 44
Operation Downfall, 86–87
Operation Overlord, 76–80
Operation Sea Lion, 40
Operation Torch, 58

Pacific Ocean, 7, 10, 51, 53, 75–76, 82

Patton, George S., 60, 62, 80
Pearl Harbor, 7–17, 21, 50–51, 54, 68, 71, 97
Philippines, 51–53, 75, 83, 84–85
Poland, 20, 30–32, 95

Red Army, 32–33, 45
refugees, 93
Rommel, Erwin, 36, 49, 57–59
Roosevelt, Franklin Delano, 17, 27, 43, 46, 51, 57, 68, 71, 75, 82, 87
Royal Air Force, 40–43

Sicily, 60–61, 62
Soviet Union, 30–33, 44–47, 51, 88, 93, 95–96
Spanish Civil War, 27, 29
spies, 10, 44, 96
Stalin, Joseph, 30–32, 33, 44, 46, 57–58, 75, 87–88, 91, 96

ABOUT THE AUTHOR

Susan E. Hamen is a full-time editor and freelance writer who finds her most rewarding career experiences to be writing children's books. She has written books on various topics, including the Wright brothers, the Industrial Revolution, and Germany. Her book *Clara Barton: Civil War Hero and American Red Cross Founder* was chosen for the ALA's 2011 Amelia Bloomer Project Book List. Hamen lives in Minnesota with her husband and two children.